DATE DUE

MAMMALS

MAMMALS

MICHAEL GEORGE
THE CHILD'S WORLD

PHOTO CREDITS
Joe McDonald: front cover
Len Rue Jr.: 11
Ralph Clevenger: 23
EarthViews/Craig Matkin: 21
Comstock/George Lepp: 2
Comstock/Bill Ervin: 19
Comstock/Phylis Greenberg: 15
Comstock/Denver Bryan: 17, 31
Comstock/Russ Kinne: back cover, 9, 13, 25, 29
Merlin D. Tuttle/Bat Conservation Int'l.: 27

Distributed to schools and libraries in the United States by
ENCYCLOPAEDIA BRITANNICA EDUCATIONAL CORP.
310 South Michigan Avenue
Chicago, Illinois 60604

Library of Congress Cataloging-in-Publication Data
George, Michael, 1964-
Mammals / by Michael George.
p.   cm.
Summary: Introduces the physical and behavioral
characteristics of various mammals, including the
dolphin, armadillo, and bat.
ISBN 0-89565-846-1
1. Mammals--Juvenile literature.   [1. Mammals.]   I. Title.
QL706.2.G46   1992   91-36374
599--dc20   CIP
                                             AC

CONTENTS

To many people, mammals are the most familiar and well-liked group of animals on earth. We, ourselves, are mammals. In being so, we have things in common with all the animals in this book.

Like people, all mammals are warm-blooded. Our body temperature stays nearly the same whether it's a hot summer day or a cold winter night. All mammals also have hair on their bodies, and most are covered with fur. Unlike insects or reptiles, which hatch from eggs, most mammals are born alive. After birth, young mammals drink their mother's milk for nourishment.

Despite these similarities, mammals differ in many ways. Armadillos are secretive and active only at night. Other mammals are active by day and are not at all shy. Bighorn sheep live on the tops of rugged mountain peaks. Blue whales, mammals that happen to be largest animals on earth, live in the deepest oceans.

From cuddly kittens to ferocious polar bears, from tiny mice to gigantic elephants, mammals are a complex and fascinating group of animals. As you look at the animals in this book, remember that you are related to them all.

MONKEYS

Monkeys share more traits with humans than any other animal. The characters shown here are rhesus monkeys, just one of the many kinds of monkeys. Rhesus monkeys perform at zoos and circuses throughout the world. Wild rhesus monkeys live in forests and deserts in Asia. Some prefer to live near village marketplaces or railway stations. These city-dwelling monkeys often raid gardens for food. They also steal food from shops and houses. When they can't find people food, rhesus monkeys eat plant roots, tree buds, and fruits.

GIRAFFES

Giraffes are the skyscrapers of the animal kingdom. Some adult giraffes are nearly as tall as a two-story house. To pump blood all the way up to its head, a giraffe's heart is the size of a pillow. Wild giraffes live on the grasslands of Africa. They feed on leaves at the tops of trees, which no other animals can reach. Giraffes have long, purple tongues. Their tongues are covered with tough, raspy skin so they can browse on thorny trees without getting pricked. Although giraffes rest often, a nap rarely lasts longer than a few minutes.

KOALAS

Although they look like fuzzy teddy bears, koalas are not bears at all. They are more closely related to kangaroos. Like female kangaroos, female koalas have pouches on their bellies. After birth, a newborn koala climbs up its mother's belly and into her pouch. Here, the pea-sized baby stays warm and drinks its mother's nourishing milk. About two months later, the young koala leaves its mother's pouch and begins to look for its own food—moist leaves and berries. Mature koalas eat and sleep in trees and rarely venture to the ground.

ARMADILLOS

Armadillos are unusual creatures that look like little armored tanks. They're covered by tough, leathery skin that protects the armadillo as it slips through dense, thorny brush. Armadillos live in the southern United States. They are also found throughout Central and South America. They sleep during the day in underground burrows. At night they forage for beetles, grubs, and ants. Armadillos have long, sharp claws that they use to dig for food. Although their sight is poor, armadillos have a keen sense of smell and hearing.

BIGHORN SHEEP

Bighorn sheep live in the high mountains of North America. They prefer steep slopes where there are few trees. Bighorn sheep can climb rocky cliffs without any trouble. They have special pads on their hooves that prevent them from slipping. Bighorn sheep feed mostly on tender grasses, flowers, and berries. Male bighorns are called *rams*. They have huge, curling horns on the sides of their heads that they use to fight over the females. Two rams crash into each other over and over until one of the sheep gives up.

ZEBRAS

Zebras live on the open grassy plains of Africa. Mature zebras are slightly smaller than horses. Zebras live in herds that may contain 10,000 animals. The herds roam across the African savannas in search of the best grass to eat. Zebras are always alert and cautious. Their main enemy, the lion, is a constant threat. Fortunately, zebras have many abilities that help them avoid lions. They have excellent eyesight and can run at speeds of up to 60 miles per hour. Lions are not nearly so fast. They usually catch only young or sick zebras.

WHALES

This humpback whale doesn't look much like the other animals in this book, but it is still a mammal. Although whales live in the ocean, they come to the surface to breathe air. Some whales can hold their breath for over an hour! Whales are the largest of all mammals. One type, the blue whale, is the largest animal that has ever lived on earth. Some of these giants weigh three times as much as the heaviest dinosaur. A blue whale's tongue alone is larger than a car! Despite their enormous size, blue whales eat only small, shrimplike creatures called *krill*.

ELEPHANTS

While whales are the largest of all animals, elephants
are the largest animals that live on land. An adult
elephant can grow as tall as a school bus and may
weigh as much as 60 men. It can eat more food
in a single day than you can eat in an entire year.
Elephants dine on tree leaves, bark, and roots. They
also eat flowers and shrubs. Elephants are so huge
that people are their only enemies. Armed with
powerful guns, hunters kill thousands of elephants
every year. They sell the elephants' tusks to make
piano keys, art, and jewelry.

POLAR BEARS

Polar bears are the main attraction at many public zoos, and rightfully so. They are one of the biggest and furriest bears in the world. Wild polar bears live in the Arctic, near the North Pole. They have a thick layer of fat, called *blubber*, beneath their fur. The blubber helps to keep them warm, even when they swim in the icy Arctic Ocean. Adult polar bears can swim as fast as a small electric boat. They eat large sea animals, such as porpoises, walruses, and seals. Polar bears have powerful legs and long, sharp claws to help them catch their dinner.

BATS

Bats are the only mammals that have wings and can fly. A bat's wings are made of tough, leathery skin. Most bats sleep during the day. They sleep in damp, dark places hanging upside down. At night, bats search for food. Bats that live in tropical areas eat fruits, flower nectar, small rodents, or fish. The infamous vampire bat prefers to suck blood from cattle and horses. Most bats that live in the United States eat flies, mosquitoes, and other insects. Bats are expert fliers. They can catch small insects even on the darkest nights.

DOLPHINS

Did you know that dolphins are a type of whale? Unlike their relatives, dolphins are not much larger than people. Dolphins can hold their breath for only about five minutes, so they do not dive very deep underwater. There are many different kinds of dolphins. One of the most familiar is the bottlenose dolphin, shown in the picture. At marine parks, trained bottlenose dolphins do tricks, leap out of the water, and play with their handlers. Dolphins are one of the most intelligent mammals. They sometimes make up their own games for fun.

WOLVES

Many people think that wolves are vicious creatures that stalk dark forests, terrorizing both man and beast. Actually, most of our ideas about wolves are not true. A wolf pack is just a family of wolves. The family works together to raise the young and hunt. Wolves prefer to eat deer, moose, or caribou. When food is scarce, they can survive on small rodents. Although many people think otherwise, wolves kill only what they can eat. Usually, they attack only the weakest or oldest animals—ones that would die soon anyway.

THE CHILD'S WORLD
NATUREBOOKS

Wildlife Library

Space Library

Adventure Library

Concord
South Side